It's Time to Live Your Life...

FULLY ALIVE!

Janice Brown Carbon, L.C.S.W.

It's Time to Live Your Life... Fully Alive!
Janice Brown Carbon, L.C.S.W.

Copyright ©2013, Janice Brown Carbon, All rights reserved

Cover image: Shutterstock.com
Cover and book design: Tau Publishing Design Department
Author Photo: Oscar Rajo

No part of this book may be reproduced, stored in a retrieval system or transmitted in any form or by any means - electronic, mechanical, photocopying, recording, or otherwise - without written permission of the publisher.

For information regarding permission, write to:
Tau Publishing, LLC
Attention: Permissions Dept.
4727 North 12th Street
Phoenix, AZ 85014

ISBN 978-1-61956-095-6

First Edition February 2013
10 9 8 7 6 5 4 3 2 1

Published and printed in the United States of America by Tau Publishing, LLC
For additional inspirational books visit us at TauPublishing.com

TauPublishing.com
Words of Inspiration

Dedicated to:
Max, Jack, Oliver, and Ellie

Acknowledgements

This book has come to publication with the help and support of many friends. First off, I would like to thank several people at Focus TV. This book came to fruition as the result of a TV program I did with them last spring. In particular I want to thank Char Vance, president of Focus TV. It was Char who first suggested that I put this information into book form. I also want to thank Mary Salzer, producer and director at Focus TV. Mary has always been so kind and patient with me. I thank her for her encouragement with this project. I want to thank Lisa Flood whose gracious and enthusiastic on-air presence helped me so much in presenting this material to a wide audience. Last, but not least, I want to thank Janie Harney for her continued support. Although it has been a huge dream of mine to write this book, it never would have seen the light of day without the tremendous encouragement I received from these good folks at Focus TV.

There are wonderful people who gave so kindly and generously of their time and expertise. I especially want to thank Fr. James Schott, Fr. Joseph Doyle, Fr. Gerard Stapleton, Sr. Paula Derise, Sylvia Thomas, Sherryl Freche, and Constance

Brown. Their prayers, along with their encouraging words and concrete suggestions, helped me tremendously.

Because of professional confidentiality, I cannot name the many wonderful clients who also took the time to read through the rough drafts of this work. Each and every suggestion they made was given serious consideration. Without them, and the many wonderful clients before them, this book would not have been possible.

I want to give special thanks to my publisher Jeff Campbell at Tau Publishing. Jeff has been extremely helpful and kind in working with this novice author. I want to thank the wonderful staff that Jeff has assembled at Tau for their professional expertise. People like my editor Patience Suriano, and graphic and book designer Lorien Sheppard have been invaluable to this project. I am blessed to have Tau as my publisher!

Let me thank the many prayer warriors, especially Beatrice Carbon, who stormed heaven with prayers in loving support of this project. I want to thank my father, Harwood Brown, for his love and support, but even more importantly, for the prayerful example he set over the years. A little girl who sees her father kneel to say his prayers never forgets that image!

I am blessed with two beautiful daughters, Stephanie delaHoussaye and Courtney Garrett, whose love and encouragement have seen me through many a life challenge. I want them to know that their enthusiastic support for this project spurred me on to finish. I dedicate this book to my precious grandchildren Max, Jack, Oliver, and Eillie. I give special thanks for them to their loving fathers, Lee and Philip. I thank these good men for their love and support.

It is my fervent prayer that this book bears good fruit; and that the fruit it bears will bring much honor and glory to God! Amen!

Table of Contents

Introduction 1

Developmental Stages of Thinking 11
The Infant Stage 13
    The Infantile Thinker 13
The Child Stage 17
    The Childish Thinker 18
The Adolescent Stage 21
    The Adolescent Thinker 21
The Adult Stage 25
    The Adult Thinker 25

Catholic Adult Thinking 33

Case Studies
Jeff and Jennifer 43
Colin 49
Cindy 55

How to Develop a Catholic Adult Paradigm 63
The Child Within 65
My Life in Context 66
Mission Statement for My Life 67
Trust in God, Not Man 68
What Would I Do If This Was Jesus? 69
Psalm 136: Trusting in God's Protection 70
An Attitude of Gratitude: How to Live in Peace and Joy 71
Scripture 72
Mass and Adoration 73
Our Lady 74
Prayer of Surrender to God, Our Father 75
Final Thought 77
Let's Stay in Touch 79

"The glory of God is man fully alive!"

-St. Irenaeus, Bishop of Lyon, 2nd century
Early Father and Doctor of the Catholic Church

Introduction

Imagine, for a moment, feeling completely free to be yourself, without any worry about what others may think. Imagine living a meaningful life that brings you peace of mind and joy in your relationships. Imagine being able to remain stress-free in this stressful world. Imagine being able to enjoy your life regardless of your circumstances.

Sound too good to be true? Not in my book! In fact, that is precisely why I am writing this little book. I want to teach you how to mature in your thinking, so that you can take back control of your life. More importantly, these are all promises made to us by God in scripture. He created us to live in emotional freedom so that we can bring glory to Him with our lives. The quote from St. Irenaeus states, "The glory of God is man fully alive!" The full context of that statement suggests that man fully alive lives glorifying God.

The Old Testament scripture Jeremiah 29:11 says, *"For I know the plans I have for you, says the Lord, plans for your welfare and not for evil, to give you a future and a hope."* How many people actually live the power of this scripture? So many people settle into small, boring, restrictive, and fearful lives; not coming close to having the life God wants them to have. How sad! It doesn't have to be this way.

I have worked with thousands of people from all walks of life in my twenty plus years as a Catholic psychotherapist with a faith based practice. I love the work I do, and the people I meet. My clients come in all ages, with all sorts of issues. Although clients come in for different reasons, I have noticed a common denominator. If there is one struggle that most of my clients have, regardless of their particular presenting problem, it is this: an emotional immaturity that keeps them trapped in ineffective ways of looking at life. By staying trapped in these immature paradigms, they are unable to step into the truth of who they are as human beings. They are unable to become the persons they were created by God to be. They are unable to tap into the wonderful plan God has for their lives. They are unable to live their lives *fully alive*!

The first part of this book will be devoted to an explanation and understanding of the developmental stages of thinking. I was first introduced to this theory of "developmental stages of thinking" by Dr. Teal Bennett in the late 1980's. At that time, Dr. Bennett was a very popular and successful psychotherapist at Tulane University Medical Center. Teal became my therapist and my mentor during this time of major transition in my life. I am forever grateful to her for the help she gave me. Teal helped me to shake the guilt and fear, and begin the process of becoming my own person. However, because our counseling was done on a strictly secular level, it got me only so far; in spite of the fact that Dr. Teal Bennett was an excellent psychotherapist.

In the many intervening years, I have modified this theory as I have used it with my own clients. The developmental stages of thinking that I will share with you now, reflect aspects of the many and varied books I have read, along with approaches I have studied. They include ideas from Stephen Covey's *Seven Habits of Highly Effective People*, as well as Cloud and Townsend's *Boundaries*, just to name a few. They also reflect many years of personal spiritual development. I share them with you now, not as the last word on how to get your life together, but more as an excellent first step.

For many years I have used this theory as a mechanism to help clients gauge the maturity of their outlook on life. A person's effectiveness in life is directly related to this emotional maturity level. These developmental stages are based on the psychological developmental stages of the human being: infant, child, adolescent, and adult, with which we are all familiar.

It is my premise that we do not achieve real emotional freedom until we reach and maintain the adult stage paradigm. It is in this adult stage that we can live *fully alive*. In order to get there we have to advance through the other stages. These stages are developmental in the sense that they build upon each other and progress in sequence. There are age appropriate behaviors and thought patterns that go along with each stage. Problems arise when we get stuck in a stage other than the adult stage. When this happens our thinking and resulting behavior is ineffective, limiting our lives and our happiness. My job, as a therapist, is to help clients assess their current maturity level, and help them make the necessary adjustments so that they can progress to the adult state, and develop an adult paradigm on life.

As we go through these different developmental stages, one of the first things that you will notice is that you can be in different stages in different areas of your life at the same time. For instance, a person can be adult in their professional life, while being quite childish in their personal relationships, and maybe even infantile with certain people who let them get away with it. Personal relationships are usually the hardest areas for most people, with family of origin relationships often being the hardest of all.

You may also notice that you can spend time in all of these stages in any single day! However, you will also notice that you really do feel better and much more confident in the adult stage paradigm.

I admit that this approach appears to be very simplistic, and in many ways it is limited in scope. However, it has proven to be extremely effective over the years that I have used it with clients. It is a great way to pinpoint where the problem exists in the client's thinking. It also gives the proper fix. This approach makes it easy to zero in, fine tune, and properly adjust immature thinking patterns.

As a former kindergarten teacher I like to keep things simple and elemental. I am also practical. This is a very simple and easy to use process. Anyone can use it and benefit from it. There is nothing new here. The information that I will share with you has been around for decades, much of it considered common knowledge. What is unique is how I use the information and apply it to help clients change their lives. The results have been remarkable. The response from my clients has been overwhelmingly positive. Lives have been turned around. People have been set free to become their best selves. Clients will state that they finally like themselves and feel good about the lives they are living. They feel like they are becoming the persons God created them to be. According to St. Irenaeus, they are living life *fully alive*. This program has worked for them, and now it can work for you.

A word of caution: this book is written in a light, easy to read style. It will be tempting to rush through it quickly. Despite its easy style, it is chocked full of useful information.

Introduction

Please give yourself time to process this information.

The book is divided into three main parts. The first part presents the theory behind the developmental stages of thinking. It culminates in the section on Catholic adult thinking. Following each section I have included reflective questions under the title "Food for Thought." These questions are designed to help the reader apply the theories presented in a personal way to their own lives. This process resembles what actually goes on in a psychotherapy session.

The second part of the book is comprised of three case studies. These are very helpful in "fleshing out" the theory presented in the first section. Case studies are another way of bringing the theoretical to life, making it real. More "Food for Thought" questions follow.

The last section contains several exercises that I use with clients, to help them in developing a Catholic adult paradigm. I suggest that you spend several days contemplating each exercise before moving on to the next one. In this way you will give yourself the opportunity to internalize the concepts presented. By following this suggestion, you will begin to feel your relationship with God grow. For some of you, it will be the beginning of living your life in a personal relationship with your Creator. For those of you who already enjoy that wonderful relationship, you will find that your relationship will deepen and expand. Your life will come into clearer focus, giving you a new sense of purpose.

Now come with me, it's time for you to live your life *fully alive*!

Developmental Stages of Thinking

> "When I was a child, I spoke like a child,
> I thought like a child, I reasoned like a child;
> when I became a man, I gave up childish ways."
>
> 1 Corinthians 13:11

Developmental Stages of Thinking

In this section I will present the different developmental stages of thinking. First I will explain the developmental stage and the appropriate corresponding behaviors for that stage; then I will explain what happens when we get stuck in each stage. Often simply hearing these descriptions and being given this information helps a client begin the process of changing perspective. This information also provides its own motivation for change. Who wants to remain a self-centered infant, a fearful child, or an angry adolescent? We all want to be principle centered adults. We all want to live in freedom and truth.

As you read through the different stages, people you know will come to mind. This will give you some insight into those relationships. However, the real power and purpose of this section is to give you the information to reflect upon your own life. Your purpose in reading this book is to improve your life. I promise that if you focus on yourself and use the information I present here and in the next sections, your life will improve greatly. Let's get started.

The Infant Stage

What do we know about the psychological development of the infant? Based on scientific evidence we know that the infant is ego-centric. This means that the infant believes that he or she is the center of the universe. In fact, for a time, the infant does not realize that other people exist! We are told that the infant has a symbiotic relationship with his or her mother for the first six months of the infant's life. What this means is that the infant does not see the mother as a separate human being with her own needs and desires. Instead, the mother is seen more as an appendage, something like a huge arm that exists only to meet the infant's needs.

We know that the infant is motivated by pleasure. Each infant is concerned with maintaining a constant state of comfort. Infants, of course, cannot meet their own needs, they need someone else (the mother) to meet those needs for them. How do they get their needs met? They scream and holler, and the mother comes running to meet the infant's needs.

The Infantile Thinker

While the above mentioned behaviors are age appropriate for

infants to two year olds, I know that there are people in their 20's, 30's, 40's, 50's, etc. that demonstrate these same behaviors. I believe that these people have an infantile paradigm on life. This outlook colors the way they look at life, and affects how they interact with other people.

These are people who are totally self-centered. They do not respect others, and act as if they are the only ones that count. In other words, like the infant, they do not seem to realize that other people exist! They lack empathy. They have a huge sense of entitlement. They worship the unholy trinity: me, myself, and I. Infantile thinkers come in different shapes and sizes. They are the narcissists, the bullies and abusers, the addicts, and "spoiled brats" to name a few.

These individuals are motivated by pleasure. It is all about what feels good in the next five minutes. Their motto is, "If it feels good, do it!" Another one is, "If I want it, I should have it!" They are very impulsive, giving no thought to consequences, including other people's feelings. They cannot, or will not, delay personal gratification. When things don't go their way, they throw a fit.

Infantile thinkers are overly controlled by their emotions. They do things when they feel like it, and only when and if they feel like it. If an infantile thinker wants to do something, he will do it no matter how hard it is to do. Likewise, if the infantile thinker does not want to do something, he will not do it no matter how easy it is to do. This limits the infantile thinker's success in life. Think about it. How many things do we do, that we do not feel like doing, simply because they are the right or necessary things to do? This trait makes infantile thinkers "fair weather friends." These people are notoriously undependable. They may be around when the going is good, but when things get tough, they bolt. You cannot count on them. They are unable to commit for the long haul.

As human beings, we were created to love people and use things. Infantile thinkers have it backwards; they love things and use people! In fact, they see other people as objects to be used for their own personal gain. These individuals do not learn to meet their own needs; they learn to manipulate others into meeting their needs for them. And, infantile thinkers will not take "no," for an answer.

Some examples of infantile thinkers would include: the celebrity who treats the people she employs with disdain; the individual with a sex addiction who sees women as objects to be used for his personal pleasure; and the social climber who cultivates friendships with only those people who can benefit him.

Hallmarks of Infantile thinking: self-centered, no empathy, pleasure seeking, controlled by emotions, impulsive, instant gratification, uses people, symbiotic, dependent, difficult to get along with, will not accept "no."

Food for Thought

When reading about infantile thinkers, who in your life comes to mind? What is it about this person that qualifies them as an infantile thinker?

How does this new information change the way you view your relationship with this person?

We all have moments when we fall into this category.

Can you identify times in your life when you adopt an infantile approach to problems?

Infantile thinkers are ruled by their feelings and lack personal discipline. Are these issues problems for you, or someone close to you? How do these problems manifest in your life? Do you, or they, struggle with addictions, over indulgences, or a short temper?

The Child Stage

This stage is based on the age appropriate behaviors for latency age development in children, roughly four to nine years old. This stage differs significantly from the Infant stage in several ways. Whereas the infant is totally self-centered, the child is other-focused. These are "the good little boys and girls". They are rule followers and people pleasers.

Remember the infant's symbiotic relationship with the mother; the infant did not know that the mother was a separate person. Well, the four year old knows only too well that the mother is separate. The four year old worries that when the mother leaves, will the mother return? This worry creates anxiety and a fear of abandonment.

Although four year olds do not articulate this, they know instinctively that they need the grownups around them to take care of them. It's a matter of life or death! They cannot survive on their own! Their motivation goes something like this, "Tell me what you want me to do, and I will work really, really hard to do a really good job, so you will love me, and take care of me, and I will be safe and secure."

The Childish Thinker

Most of my clients see themselves stuck in this stage. They are good people who do their best to follow the rules and be good citizens. They are peace lovers who are conflict avoidant, and willing to accommodate others. They are also unhappy, and living in guilt and fear.

They often manifest codependent behaviors. They believe they can make and keep other people happy; and they are willing to go to extreme lengths to accomplish this end. These folks have trouble saying, "no." They routinely give away their personal power to others. After a while, they begin to run on empty. Because they define themselves in terms of other people, they do not have a keen sense of self. They constantly worry about what others think of them. This addiction to approval creates a sense of lingering guilt, as they worry that they have not done a good enough job. Some of their biggest fears can be summed up as, "don't yell at me, don't be angry with me, and whatever you do, don't leave me!"

By the time these childish thinkers come into my office they are emotionally and physically exhausted. They are often bitter and confused. They honestly do not understand why their personal goodness is not bringing them success nor happiness. They are upset when they look around and see that others, who are not as kind or caring, appear to be much happier. It seems so unfair. They are confused and discouraged. Their lives are not working well for them. They are becoming angry and bitter. It is this anger that will move them into the next stage, the Adolescent Stage.

Some of the people that would fall into the childish thinking category include: people pleasers, rule followers, codependent people, burned out individuals. Examples of some childish thinkers would include: the parent who spoils the teen, trying to keep her happy; the wife and mother who has devoted her life to her family and has lost all sense of herself; the employee whose sole motivation is to keep the boss happy all the time.

Hallmarks of Childish thinking: other focused, people pleaser, rule follower, peace loving, conflict avoidant, motivated by fear and guilt, gives away personal power, good heart, insecure, compliant, easy to get along with, has trouble saying "no".

Food for thought

Who in your life qualifies as a childish thinker?

If you are a childish thinker, how are you giving away your personal power? To whom are you giving away your personal power?

How does chronic people pleasing keep you mired in fear and guilt?

What could you accomplish in your life if you could learn to hold on to your personal power? In other words, what could you accomplish if you could get past the need for constant approval?

The Adolescent Stage

As the name implies, this is age appropriate behavior for teens. The driving motivation of this stage is anger. Remember the child, being motivated by fear, says, "Tell me what you want me to do and I will do a really, really good job…" The adolescent, motivated by anger says, "Tell me what you want me to do, and I will make sure I don't do it!" "You can't make me do it!"

Anger is energizing. Because of this energy, adolescents think they are independent, but they are not. Adolescents are what I call counter dependent. They are not really free. They are reactive, rebelling against authority. Adolescents are tired of doing what others want them to do. They want to be independent, but they need to pass through this stage first.

The Adolescent Thinker

When childish thinkers get tired of having to please others all the time, they get angry and start to rebel. This is often an uncomfortable feeling for the conflict avoidant, peace loving childish thinker. When this happens I remind them that they are actually taking a developmental step forward. In fact, it is the anger that gets them to break through their fear. This anger is essential to their progress.

This anger brings energy and confidence instead of fear. Their new internal dialogue goes something like this, "You can yell at me, you can stay angry with me, you can even leave me. I don't care! In fact, I will leave you first!" These folks have trouble accepting "no," but no trouble saying "no."

Clients seeking marriage counseling often enter therapy at this stage. These clients also highlight how people often yo-yo between the child and adolescent stages. I can hear it clearly with the words they use. The husband, for instance, may come in saying that he doesn't care anymore. He is angry and frustrated and ready to leave the marriage. He will go on to tell me how he used to care. He will let me know what a good husband he used to be. He will list all the things he used to do to make his wife happy. He will tell me that it didn't work. He's tired of trying. He's angry and bitter, and ready to give up.

Can you pick up on the angry adolescent thinking in the above paragraph? Do you also hear the childish thinker who has burned out from the impossible job of trying to keep another person happy? Very often couples have gone back and forth between these two stages of thinking several times before they come in for counseling. It goes something like this: they are hurt and angry and talk about breaking up. When their anger subsides, they decide to work things out. They commit to work harder at being better spouses, hoping to make each other happier. As before, this does not work. They become frustrated and start to threaten divorce again. Believe it or not, there are couples who live for years this way. As you might imagine, it is a miserable and frustrating existence.

Going back to the husband in the example above, my job, as the therapist, is to help him move into the adult stage of thinking, where he can become his own person, free to make a proactive, principle centered decision.

Because people in the adolescent stage are motivated by anger, it can be a dangerous time. Decisions can be impulsive and damaging. Individuals that get trapped in this stage for an extended period of time can also revert back to the infant stage. They become pleasure seeking, often using and abusing others along the way. They care about nothing and no one, but themselves!

As I have just explained, there are two possible dysfunctional outcomes to this adolescent stage of thinking. The first is the yo-yo trap, where the person goes back and forth between the child and adolescent stages. This often happens when the fear of the childish thinker reemerges. Remember, at heart, this is a fear of abandonment. Often these folks simply cannot imagine making it on their own. They are too afraid.

The other dysfunctional outcome is where the adolescent thinker reverts back to the infant stage, and stops caring about other people altogether. People can spend years stuck in their own self-centeredness. This can have profoundly negative consequences, not only for the individual, but for everyone in this person's life. Infantile thinkers often leave a trail of victims in their wake.

Hallmarks of Adolescent thinking: motivated by anger, oppositional, reactive, no respect for authority, claims not to care, self-defeating, insecure, difficult, will not accept "no," has no trouble saying "no"

Food for thought

Who is the adolescent thinker in your life?

Who or what is this person rebelling against? Describe their self-defeating behavior.

My job, as a therapist, is to help clients achieve the functional outcome of reaching the adult stage of thinking. It is as an adult thinker that the client finally comes into his own, and becomes emotionally free to be himself. The goal is to be an adult thinker in every area of life. Then life starts to get better, much better!

The Adult Stage

Adults are motivated by principles, values, and beliefs. These beliefs include religious beliefs. Adults make decisions based on maintaining their own self-respect and personal integrity. Adults are able to delay gratification. Adults are proactive. No longer in a reactive, knee jerk mode, they are able to consider the response they want to give. Adults have a keen sense of who they are as individuals. They no longer give away their personal power. These folks can accept "no" for an answer. They can also tell others "no" when necessary. They are no longer controlled by their emotions; and they are no longer addicted to other people's approval. Adults are independent. They create their own trajectory in life.

The Adult Thinker

Adult thinking requires the ability to think abstractly. This ability sets in during puberty. I have worked with clients as young as eleven and twelve years old that I was able to help by introducing this concept of adult-like thinking. It has been very effective. I believe we need to encourage young people as soon as they are able to develop this paradigm on life. Unfortunately, young people today live in a celebrity culture that actually glorifies infantile thinking and a self-centered approach to life. This is reaping tragic consequences!

When I am working with a client I explain each of the other stages: infant, child, and adolescent; then I explain adult thinking in this way. Thinking like an adult is similar to thinking like a child, but with a crucial difference. This is the difference: I am now the person whose approval I need to seek and maintain. This does not mean that I give in to infantile thinking. This is not about what I feel like doing. This requires the maturity to think abstractly and consider, "What kind of person am I?" "What kind of person do I really want to be?" "What are my values?" "What are my beliefs?" "What are my priorities in life?"

The answers to these questions then become my true north on my own personal moral compass. No matter how crazy or hectic life gets, I can find my way. I need to make decisions that are congruent with these core values and beliefs. I need to make decisions based on maintaining my own self-respect and personal integrity. I need to be true to myself. I am motivated by principles. "What is the right thing for me to do?"

I no longer give away my personal power to other people. I am no longer motivated by seeking their approval. I am no longer motivated by guilt. I am able to set appropriate personal boundaries, and an interesting thing happens. When I cease seeking approval from others, and am faithful to my principles, I become authentically me! In time, I begin to get respect from other people. Respect allows me to hold on to my personal power, whereas seeking approval diminishes my personal power. I want respect, not approval! I do not have to seek respect, it is a by-product of living an authentic and principle centered life.

Examples of adult thinking include: the person who helps those less fortunate; a father who sacrifices to provide for his family; an employee who gives a full day's work for the full day's pay.

Hallmarks of Adult thinking: principle centered, values and belief driven, moral compass, true to self, authentic, secure, self-respect, personal integrity, personal power, can accept "no," can say "no," sets appropriate boundaries, delays gratification, proactive, independent, creates own trajectory

Food for thought

Who are the strong adult thinkers in your life?

What sets these people apart for the others?

Where in your life are you already living from an adult paradigm?

Where are you still struggling to reach this adult outlook on life?

Let us now take a look at what it means to be an adult thinker as a Catholic.

Catholic Adult Thinking

"'Teacher, which is the great commandment in the law?' And he said to him, 'You shall love the Lord your God with all your heart, and with all your soul, and with all your mind. This is the great and first commandment. And a second is like it, You shall love your neighbor as yourself. On these two commandments depend all the law and the prophets.'"

Matthew 22:36-40

Catholic Adult Thinking

Because adult thinking is based on principles, values, and beliefs, let us take a look at some of the core beliefs we hold as Catholics.

Jesus said that the whole of the law could be summed up in two commands: Love God above all things with your whole heart, soul, and mind; and love your neighbor as yourself. This means that, as Catholics, we want to keep God uppermost in our hearts and minds. It also means that we are to care for others the same way we would care for ourselves. This implies a motive to serve others.

If we look at John's gospel, at the Last Supper, Our Lord says, *"A new commandment I give you, that you love one another; even as I have loved you, that you also love one another. By this all men will know that you are my disciples, if you have love for one another."* (John 13:34-35)

This command to love others is central to Our Lord's message to us. He calls us out of ourselves. He calls us to reach out to others. We are able to do this only if we put God first in our lives. So this is the basis of living ***fully alive: we put God first in our lives, and then we serve others.***

I firmly believe that this call to serve others is possible only with the grace of God. We receive this grace by putting God first, at the center of our lives. If we try to serve others without the benefit of God's grace, we fall into the trap of using others for our own gain. It becomes about how good we are to give to others. This is not the message from Our Lord. ***It is only by the grace of God that I am able to live my life for <u>His</u> Glory and not for my own glory!***

It is very important that we understand that we are not to use other people for self-gain (infantile thinking). We are also not to put others on a pedestal, where we turn them into false gods seeking their approval (childish thinking).

Let us take a moment to look at another scripture, one that might cause confusion. In the gospel of Matthew, chapter 18 begins this way: *"At that time the disciples came to Jesus saying, 'Who is the greatest in the kingdom of heaven?' And calling to him a child, he put him in the midst of them, and said, 'Truly, I say to you, unless you turn and become like children, you will never enter the kingdom of heaven. Whoever humbles himself like this child is the greatest in the kingdom of heaven."* (Matthew 18:1-4)

When I reflect on what Jesus is saying in this passage, I see that He is asking us to rely on God the way a little child relies on its parent. In other words, He is telling us that we are created to be dependent on God. We are not created to get through this life under our own steam. We are not designed to live our lives independently, apart from God. We are created to need God in our lives, the way a child needs a parent to care for them.

God wants to be God in our lives! He has created us with a desperate need for Him. We need to put Him at the center of our lives. This is why our lives do not go well when we leave Him out of the equation. In fact, left to our own devices, we all self-destruct, because then life becomes all about us!

Little children are not meant to get through this life all on their own. And we are not created to get through our lives without God. This scripture is all about the first commandment Jesus gives. Jesus tells us that we are to love God above all things, with our whole heart and mind. God has to be the most important thing in our lives. He has to be at the center!

This is a very different concept from the dysfunctional thinking patterns of the infantile and childish thinkers. Both of these involve dependence on other people. God has created us to become independent of other people (adult thinking) so that we can enter into a healthy interdependent state, where we can help each other. In order for us to successfully do this, we must stay dependent on Him, regardless of our age. We will never outgrow our need for God! The more we mature in our faith, the more we become aware of this need, and the more we lean on Him.

Let me restate what I have just said. I believe that we need to achieve **a healthy emotional independence from other people**, and **a healthy emotional dependence on God**. This is the requirement to achieve a Catholic adult paradigm. This is the requirement to live life *fully alive*!

Our Lord's message makes it clear that we are to live for God and for others. This is in sharp contrast to living a life of self-gratification and self-promotion. Unfortunately, we live in a world that promotes the glorification of self. This focus is contrary to God's plan for our lives! Is it any wonder that so many of us feel lost, depressed, and discouraged by life?

Let me again underscore the fact that we are created by God to live our lives fully reliant on Him! As we grow in our trust of God, we learn to entrust our lives to Him. We are then set free to become our true selves. We are free to become the persons He created us to be. We are then given the grace to love others.

We are finally free to live *fully alive*!

Living *fully alive* is not about chasing an adrenaline rush! It is not about jumping out of airplanes, or climbing mountains, or driving fast cars. **Living *fully alive* is about living a life that brings glory to God.** Jesus tells us that to do this we must: put God first in all things, and love others as we love ourselves.

This approach to life is radical. It changes everything! It sets you free! It gives you courage to do things that make a difference. You are finally able to live *fully alive*!

Hallmarks of Catholic Adult thinking: love of God; trust in God's love, protection, and provision; leans on God; love of neighbor; desire to serve; all hallmarks of adult thinking: principle centered; values and belief driven; moral compass; true to self; authentic; secure; self-respect; personal integrity; personal power; can accept "no"; can say "no"; sets appropriate boundaries; delays gratification; proactive; independent; creates own trajectory.

Food for thought

How does your life reflect Christ's teaching to love God above all, and to love others as yourself?

How do you put God at the center of your life?

In what ways do you serve others with your life?

How does your life glorify God?

Perhaps the best way to get a real feel for these different developmental stages of thinking is to look at some case studies. The following case studies are completely fictitious. They were made up in order to highlight the different developmental stages. The "clients" are not real people. However, their stories are very real, and highlight the developmental stages of thinking. As you read their stories think about the self-centeredness of the infantile thinker, the fear and guilt of the childish thinker, and the anger of the adolescent thinker. Then see what it takes to become a Catholic adult thinker.

Let me remind you that issues can get resolved in a few paragraphs of a case study. However, these same issues can often take many months to resolve in real life. That said, the personal growth process I describe in these case studies is realistic, and is based on the work I've done with clients over these many years.

Let's see how these "clients" learn to live *fully alive.*

Case Studies

> "…I came that they may have life,
> and have it more abundantly."
>
> John 10:10

Case Study: Jeff and Jennifer

Jennifer, 38, is a striking beauty. She is married to Jeff. Jeff, 42, is a very successful real estate broker. They have been married for 15 years. They have no children. Jeff used to talk about having children, but Jennifer says that she is not the motherly type. They met in college when Jennifer was elected sweetheart of Jeff's fraternity. Jeff was serving as president of the fraternity at the time. While both were dating other people when they met, their attraction was immediate and powerful. They broke off their former relationships and became the power couple they continue to be today.

They come into counseling because Jeff, in his words, wants to "reign in Jennifer's out of control spending." Jeff is a successful real estate broker. He used to make close to a million dollars a year and he never complained about Jennifer's spending until recently. The downturn in the economy has affected their financial situation. Jeff's income is down and so is their investment portfolio. Jeff and Jennifer live a very lavish lifestyle, and Jennifer's eight thousand dollar a month Visa bill has become a problem. Their living expenses are now exceeding Jeff's ability to provide. Jeff is borrowing money against their holdings to keep up with Jennifer's spending. Jeff initiates the counseling, hoping that I can get Jennifer to cut back her spending, just for a while, until the economy picks up. In the meantime, can Jennifer keep her Visa to four thousand dollars a month?

When I meet with this couple, Jeff talks first. He begins by explaining how very successful he is. He then goes into an explanation of how his business has been affected by the collapse of the housing market. It is obvious that it pains him to admit that money is tight. He has always prided himself on being able to give Jennifer anything and everything she wants. It is obvious that this marriage has never been a partnership between two psychological adults, but a relationship configured more like a parent and child. Now that times are tough, Jeff is asking Jennifer to be his partner (adult). He is hoping she can understand his (their) situation and cooperate with him through this tough time.

When Jennifer has a chance to respond, she acts as though she has not heard a word about their financial position. Instead Jennifer goes on about how mean Jeff has become. She shows no understanding at all, and even starts to cry when she talks about the new car she is supposed to be getting this year. She cries because she cannot believe that Jeff is going to break his promise to her like this. Jeff gets visibly uncomfortable and starts to offer ways they may be able to get her a car after all. However, it may not be the hundred thousand dollar car she has picked out. At that thought Jennifer gets visibly angry and insists that it has to be the car she wants or nothing at all. There will be no compromise here.

Let me give you my assessment of this fictitious couple, Jennifer and Jeff, based on the information I have given. It is easy to see that Jennifer acts like a spoiled brat. She has

Case Study: Jeff and Jennifer

no empathy for her husband. She has a symbiotic relationship with him similar to the one described between the infant and its mother. Jeff is the giver and Jennifer is the taker. This is how their relationship works. As long as Jeff can give and Jennifer can take, things work well for them. Jennifer also seems to love things (car), and uses people (Jeff). She has no thought to consequences or other people's feelings. Her tears are manipulation to get what she wants. When she doesn't get what she wants, she throws a fit. Jennifer is a classic infantile thinker.

Now let me give you my thoughts about Jeff. Although Jeff has been taking a pseudo-parental role with Jennifer, he is actually a childish thinker. Jeff is a successful rule follower and people pleaser. His ability to read and please people, has probably contributed to his tremendous success in business. Childish thinkers want to please the people important to them. It is obvious from the interaction described that Jeff has taken on the job of making and keeping Jennifer happy. He appears to have been able to accomplish this, keeping her happy for many years. However, circumstances change, as they always do. This successful businessman has been giving away his personal power for years. He has been settling for Jennifer's approval in order to feel good about himself. Under the current circumstances, Jennifer is withholding her approval. She is not about to support him during this stressful time. She is concerned only about maintaining her own comfort level. She insists on remaining comfortable at any and all cost. Jeff is beginning to burn out. He is starting to feel frustrated and angry. It will not be long before bitterness sets in.

Jeff has been operating as a childish thinker in his marriage to Jennifer. For fifteen years he prided himself on being able to treat her like a queen. There was nothing he would not do for his wife. It is only because of circumstances beyond his control, the downturn in the economy, that things have changed so drastically. Left to himself, Jeff would continue to "spoil" Jennifer. I want to stress an important point here; taking on the job of keeping another person happy never works! Never ever!

What would typically happen with a couple like this is that Jennifer would not continue with counseling. Like most infantile thinkers, she refuses to accept any responsibility for her life, and has no desire to change her life in any way. And the reason she would use to stop the sessions would be that she did not want to spend the money! Jennifer would also become angry that Jeff continues. And Jeff probably would continue the counseling because he needs support from somewhere, and he will not get it from Jennifer.

Jeff is going to go through a very stressful period that will require a lot of self-reflection and tough decisions. The sessions will allow him to blow off steam and share some of his concerns. Jeff could get angry enough to want to end his marriage. Or he could act out his anger by having an affair. Jeff will have to move beyond the anger at himself and at Jennifer. He will have to move past the feelings of powerlessness over the economy, as well as the powerlessness he feels in his marriage.

My focus with Jeff would be to help him develop an adult paradigm. I would ask Jeff the important questions about his values, beliefs, and priorities. What does Jeff believe about marriage? The answer to this question would set a course for Jeff to follow to restructure his relationship with Jennifer. This will not be an easy task, and it will take time. But Jeff can learn to set appropriate boundaries and make decisions that maintain his self-respect and personal integrity.

Marriages are tricky because there is another person involved who has their own agenda. In this case Jennifer is a narcissist.

Narcissists rarely change. I suspect that in this case Jennifer would decide to stay married to Jeff. Jennifer will never want to take care of herself. Jeff can still give her a nice enough life, so she will not leave.

By becoming an adult thinker Jeff decides to stay in the marriage in order to honor his marriage vows. He sees himself as a generous person who likes to do nice things for his wife. However, he is no longer controlled by seeking Jennifer's approval. He is not easily manipulated. He is clear about what he wants to do, and he holds the line. Jeff has taken the steps to shut down the credit cards, and has gone to a strict cash system with Jennifer. He may be disappointed in his marriage, but he is feeling much better about himself.

Jeff is growing in his faith. With his life in shambles, Jeff has been brought to his knees. He has turned to God in prayer. In fact, he sets aside time every day for prayer and reflection on scripture. When things were good for Jeff, his attendance at Sunday Mass was sporadic. Now Jeff has become much more faithful in his attendance. As a result, he has been invited to join a men's prayer group. This group meets for daily Mass one day a week. They are also involved in organizing help for those in need. Recently, Jeff helped spearhead an initiative to get major supplies donated and delivered to a neighboring community that was devastated by a tornado.

By nature Jeff is a giver. He will continue to find ways to give, ways that help others and bring glory to God. Jeff loves Jennifer, but his life has expanded beyond the miserable task of trying to keep her happy. Jeff has begun to live his life *fully alive*.

Food for thought

How did Jeff give away his personal power to Jennifer?

What did Jeff need to do to get his personal power back?

Can you name two things Jeff did to begin to live his life *fully alive*? (Hint: How does Jeff's life bring glory to God?)

Case Study: Colin

Colin is a 21 year old college student. He has just been put on academic probation for a poor GPA. This is the third college Colin has attended since high school. Colin failed out of two previous colleges. Colin's parents insist that he get into counseling to figure out why he continues to sabotage himself.

Colin is the fourth of five children. Colin is the fourth son; he has a sister a year younger than himself. Colin's older brothers are very successful. The oldest brother is an attorney. The second brother is finishing up his MBA. The third brother is a computer genius with an awesome job, making great money. The first two brothers are married, the third brother is engaged. Colin's sister has just been accepted to medical school. Colin is on his way to failing out of his third college.

Colin considers himself the black sheep of the family. He feels closer to his mom than to his dad. Colin's dad has a very successful insurance business. His dad is also very controlling and domineering. Colin and his dad go head to head all the time. Colin states that he hates his dad, and that it is his dad that is the problem. Colin is convinced that his life would be in good shape if only his dad would just get off his back and leave him alone.

When I meet with Colin I begin to hear the story of a young boy who felt lost and overlooked in his family. While growing up, Colin envied the relationships he observed between his brothers and his dad. No matter what the older boys did, his dad seemed to be pleased. They would spend time together with sports and fishing. Colin was not as good at sports and too young to join in the fishing. No matter what Colin tried to do, it was never good enough for his dad.

Colin felt closer to his mom. She was not as critical as his dad. But his mom seemed more interested in his younger sister. They would spend time doing girl things that did not interest him. Colin felt alienated and invisible in his own home.

Colin started sneaking alcohol when he was thirteen. His freshman year in high school he started smoking marijuana. His grades started to fall. Colin's high school grades were very mediocre. He was smart enough to barely scrape by without much studying. He failed out his first year away at college. Having developed no personal discipline, he partied hard, and slept through too many classes. His parents were angry and disappointed.

Then Colin enrolled in a junior college. His parents thought that this would be a way for him to raise his GPA and mature a bit. Colin hated the place and hardly attended any classes. Colin spent most days smoking weed. Colin's grades were even worse this time. Colin spent the rest of the year working at a restaurant bussing tables.

After staying out of school for a year, Colin enrolled in a third college, one where his dad had some pull to get him admitted. This is his "last chance." His personal discipline, however, is still lacking, and so are his grades. It is at this point that he comes in for counseling.

My assessment of Colin is that he is stuck in the adolescent stage of thinking. Colin is oppositional to authority, especially his dad. Colin does not have a healthy sense of himself. He has no real experience with personal success in life. He only knows failure. Therefore, he has not discovered his strengths as a person. Colin is self-defeating. He is stuck in a self-destructive cycle. He has not achieved personal autonomy. My task, as his therapist, is to help Colin move into the adult stage of thinking.

As we go through the developmental stages of thinking together, Colin can see that he is self-indulgent like the infant. And like the infant, he has no personal discipline or self-control. He has been motivated by pleasure, and has been very short-sighted. He can also see that he has given up on pleasing his parents, especially his father. After spending years as a child trying to get his father's attention, he has simply given up. This giving up came about because of his anger at his dad. Colin moved from a childish paradigm to an adolescent paradigm. Over time his anger has developed into a simmering rage. Now Colin's decisions are motivated by anger and pleasure seeking. Colin is one of those people that reverted back to the infantile thinking paradigm after getting stuck in the adolescent stage.

Colin's breakthrough comes when he admits that he continues to make bad decisions and avoid good decisions. He acknowledges that he does this because he thinks that if he chose the good decisions, his dad would win! This is a major breakthrough! Colin has been making bad decisions in an attempt to punish his dad. If Colin can begin to see how self-defeating this approach to life really is, he can begin to turn his life around. Progress begins when Colin can admit that he does, in fact, want a good life for himself. He knows that to get that life, he has to make wise decisions. He knows that his dad also wants him to make wise decisions. The challenge for Colin is this: can he separate his dad out from the decision making all together? Can Colin get a sense of the kind of person he really wants to be? Can he get excited about the kind of life he wants to have? What are his values, beliefs, and priorities? In other words, Colin needs to take ownership of his own life. He needs to start taking personal responsibility for his decisions.

Once Colin takes his father out of the equation, he stops rebelling. Before long, he begins to make better decisions. In time he quits smoking weed, and he starts to take school seriously. Colin's GPA improves. He aces an accounting course. This opens up the possibility for a career in accounting. For the first time in his life, Colin experiences personal success. He begins to see that he has unique strengths and talents. For the first time, Colin can glimpse a life for himself as an adult, a successful adult! This is another major breakthrough for Colin.

In time, Colin begins to pull away from his "loser" friends. He joins a Catholic singles group at the suggestion of a fellow student from his study group. There he meets people who share his values and beliefs. The group meets monthly for Mass and Adoration. For the first time in his life Colin sees Mass as a positive experience. He actually looks forward to Sunday Mass now. Most importantly, Colin begins to develop a personal relationship with God that deepens quickly through his time spent in Adoration. Colin also begins to date.

Colin is beginning to feel much better about himself now that he has direction in his life. His confidence is growing with his personal achievements. Colin is learning to live life based on maintaining his own self-respect and personal integrity. He is able to reach outside of himself and form relationships with other people. He is making new friends. Through the singles group, Colin gets involved in outreach programs that help the needy. Colin likes the person he has become. He is creating his own trajectory in life. Colin finally feels comfortable in his own skin.

As Colin's life continues to improve; his father begins to take notice. Colin's willingness to take responsibility for his own life has allowed him to stop blaming his father for all of his own shortcomings. Colin is also able to forgive his father for not being able to understand him earlier. In fact, things have improved to the point that he and his father have started to spend time together. Colin has even gone on a fishing trip with his dad. Colin likes his life. He is living his life *fully alive*.

Food for thought

What relationship is at the root of Colin's self-sabotaging behavior?

What does Colin need to do to get himself free?

What does Colin do to develop his relationship with God?

How does Colin reach out in love to others?

How does Colin's life glorify God?

Case Study: Cindy

Cindy is a 62 year old grandmother. Cindy has been married to David for 40 years. David is also 62 and will be retiring from his job in three years. They have two children and three grandchildren. Cindy has been a stay at home mom. She has also been the primary caregiver for her grandson Noah who is now 3 years old. Noah's mom is Cindy's daughter April. Noah's dad left when Noah was a baby, and so April has to work. Cindy and David have helped April and Noah out financially. They gave April the down payment for her home. They also gave April Cindy's old car when it was time to trade it in. April has a good job, but always seems to need financial bailouts. April also likes going out with her friends on weekends. This means that Noah is with Cindy and David every weekend he is not with his father.

Cindy's son Matt is married with two children. Matt has a great job. He and his family live out of state. Cindy does not get to see him or his children as much as she would like. Cindy is happy for Matt's success, but she feels bad that April's life has not gone as well.

Cindy comes into counseling because she is unhappy and

angry all the time. She loves her husband and sees how blessed her life has been, but Cindy is miserable inside. She is burned out and dreading what David's retirement will bring. David has started to complain that Cindy is never available to him. David loves his grandson Noah, but he is starting to resent Cindy's constant involvement.

Cindy's story is a familiar one for many women her age. Cindy is a childish thinker who has lost the sense of who she is. Cindy is a good-hearted person. She is giving and peace loving. These are wonderful traits. But when you have lost all sense of yourself, in other words, when you have lost your self-respect and personal integrity, you begin to feel used and abused. Things are out of balance. The tail is wagging the dog!

Cindy's life is out of balance because, as a childish thinker, she has been trying to keep her daughter April happy. April shows traits of infantile thinking. She will continue to take and take. Cindy is going to have to learn to set the appropriate boundaries with April. This will become easier as she develops an adult paradigm. As Cindy reflects on her own values, beliefs, and priorities, she is able to see better options for herself. She is then able to make better choices. Not only that, as good decisions encourage other good decisions, it not only gets better, but easier and easier in the process.

In counseling Cindy learns that she has been operating out of guilt and fear. She sees that she has taken on the impossible task of trying to equalize April's life with that of her brother Matt. This has put a huge burden on Cindy, and one that she is happy to finally let go.

Cindy has a very close bond with Noah since she has been his primary caregiver. While nothing will diminish Cindy's love for Noah, she needs to remind herself that she is the grandmother. Cindy will become happier as she lets go of her expectation that April should parent Noah the way she would. She needs to embrace her grandparent relationship with Noah. This will get easier because Noah will begin a nursery school program soon. Now Cindy can plan special things to do with Noah when he visits. Cindy no longer feels that she has to live her life "on call" for April.

This has freed her up so that she can spend time with her husband David. David and Cindy are finally enjoying their life together. They have plans to visit their son Matt and his family. Now Cindy is actually looking forward to David's retirement. For their entire lives they have worked hard, and saved. They envision an enjoyable future together.

Cindy is much happier now. She is clear about who she is, and she likes the person she has become. As she begins to live life congruent with her core values, she begins to live in the freedom of God's love, and the chronic guilt and fear vanish. Cindy has always had a strong prayer life. Now that she has more time to herself, she has started to attend daily Mass. David joins her when he can. She prays for her children and grandchildren, and thanks God for the many blessings in her life. Cindy has joined a women's group in her parish that reaches out to the elderly. Cindy now volunteers to cook meals for the homebound in her parish. Cindy is living her life *fully alive*.

Food for thought

What was making Cindy so miserable in her life?

What impossible task had she taken on?

What change in thinking needed to take place in order for Cindy to get free?

Name some ways that Cindy's life glorifies God?

How to Develop a Catholic Adult Paradigm

"Therefore do not be anxious, saying, 'What shall we eat?' or 'What shall we drink?' or 'What shall we wear?' For the Gentiles seek all these things; and your heavenly Father knows that you need them all. But seek first the kingdom and his righteousness, and all these things shall be yours as well. Therefore do not be anxious about tomorrow, for tomorrow will be anxious for itself. Let the day's own trouble be sufficient for the day."

Matthew 6:31-34

How to Develop a Catholic Adult Paradigm

As an adult thinker, I am expected to rise above the self-centeredness of the infant, the fear and guilt of the child, and the anger of the adolescent. I am expected to live a life based on my principles, values, and beliefs. In order to do this I need to consider what these core principles, values and beliefs are.

In a previous section I defined the Catholic adult paradigm as resting on two particular principles: loving God with my whole heart and mind, and loving others as I love myself. These are the commandments given to us directly by Our Lord, Himself.

It is the premise of this book that it is only by living a life based on these two principles that we are able to bring glory to God. In other words, it is only by living a life based on these principles that we are able to live *fully alive*!

It has also been established in the previous section that the second command, to love others as myself; flows from the first, to love God with my whole heart and mind. In other words, I can authentically serve others only with the grace of God. The way I obtain that grace is by loving God with my whole heart and mind.

In this section, I want to share with you exercises that are designed to help you put God at the center of your life. This is another way of saying that they will help you to love God with your whole heart and mind. Again, it is so important that we learn how to do this because this is how we obtain the grace necessary to be able to serve others.

These are the same exercises I use in my practice with clients. They are based on things that I have found helpful in my own spiritual journey. While I know that each of the following exercises has value, you will find yourself drawn to some more than others. I suggest that you read and consider each exercise presented below, and begin to implement them by integrating them into your life.

After reading this section through, I suggest that you take one exercise and spend a week focusing on it. Make that scripture or prayer a part of your life. The time and effort it takes will be worth it. The results will amaze you! Behavioral scientists say that it takes twenty-one days to change a habit. That is a mere three weeks. With a little effort, you can see significant change in your life within a month's time. Sticking with this program even longer will bring even greater results. You will begin to implement a real change in your life style.

You will begin to think differently about yourself and your life. You will begin to feel an inner strength emerge. You will begin to develop a sense of well-being that remains constant regardless of the circumstances in your life. In time you will begin to live in unshakable peace and joy. This is the life God has planned for you. Are you getting excited? Let's get started.

The Child Within

I often have clients bring in a picture of themselves as a young child. I want a picture that they relate to in some way. I have them look through all available pictures of themselves as children. I want a picture from around the age of three. Babies are adorable, but I want a picture a little older. I want one that shows the budding personality of the client. I want a picture that captures "the essence" of the client as a person. I want a picture from a time before the client got too discouraged and beaten up by life.

I have the client bring the chosen picture to a session. They tell me why they have chosen this particular picture. We talk about the picture. When and where was the picture taken? Can they remember that time or place? What are their memories? Then I ask them, how do they relate to their younger self? What thoughts and feelings does the picture evoke? Do they see any personality traits in the picture that are present today? Or have they, over time, lost the emotions they expressed so freely as a child? How do they feel about the little child they see? Do they see the beauty and innocence present in the child? Is there anything they want the child to know? Do they have anything to say to the child?

I tell them to frame the picture and hang it where they can easily see it every day. I encourage them to tell the child every day that they will be watching out for the child. That little child now has someone working day and night to make sure they get what they need, and keep them out of harm's way. In other words, they are making a solemn promise to themselves, a promise to take better care of themselves.

This exercise is particularly powerful in helping clients with low self-esteem. They can get in touch with their innate lovability. They learn to like themselves. They can begin to reclaim positive personality traits, forgotten talents, and personal strengths. They realize they were created to live a good and healthy life. They also realize they have something of value to offer the world. They can learn to parent themselves, to make up for any lack of love and support they may have experienced as a child. This is very important for clients who were abused as children. It is never too late to get good parenting!

This exercise has a paradoxical effect. (I will use the feminine in this example but this exercise is every bit as powerful for men.) As the client begins to relate to herself as a child, she begins to see herself as the adult. As she sees herself as the precious child she once was, she knows that she is no longer at that stage in her life. She is able to reclaim the best of her "essence" while allowing herself to mature into the adult state of mind. She begins to feel stronger and stronger as an adult. Formation of the adult paradigm is now under way!

My Life in Context

Why am I here? What is my purpose? I took the name of this book from a famous quotation of St. Irenaeus, "The glory of God is man fully alive." This quotation is cited in the Catholic Catechism, in section 294 on creation. The catechism says that **God created the world out of His goodness in order to magnify His glory**. As a part of that world, **I was created to magnify God's glory with my life**.

If we take a moment and think about the magnificent beauty that surrounds us in nature; from snow-capped mountain ranges, to tropical rain forests, to vast oceans teeming with life; we glimpse God's glory. If we look to the heavens, especially at night, we can see the stars and planets. Again, we are filled with awe at the thought of the Creator who set this all in motion. All of creation shouts out with the glory of God! As the pinnacle of His creation, mankind was created to glorify God as well. Each of us has a unique role to play in God's plan. Each of us is called to glorify God in our own special and distinct way. This is what St. Irenaeus meant when he said, "The glory of God is man fully alive." We are not *fully alive* unless we are glorifying God with our lives. This is our ultimate purpose.

By keeping my life in this larger context, I am able to rise above my petty self-centeredness. St. Paul says in Ephesians 1:4 that the thought of me (and you) was in the mind of God at the foundation of the world. Wow! This means that the thought of each of us was with God as he set the sun and stars in place! I am not here by accident! I have a noble purpose for my life! And so do you! We are created to give glory to God with our lives! We are created to live *fully alive*!

Mission Statement For My Life

I don't remember when I first ran across the "Prayer of St. Francis", but I instantly related to the words, and longed in my heart for my life to reflect the love shown through them. This prayer has served as my personal mission statement long before I went into the counseling profession. It is also the perfect mission statement for my counseling practice. While most Catholics are familiar with the prayer as a hymn we sing at Mass, I include it here for your consideration as a personal mission statement.

Prayer of St. Francis

Lord, make me a channel of your peace.
Where there is hatred, let me sow love;
where there is injury, pardon;
where there is doubt, faith;
where there is despair, hope;
where there is darkness, light;
and where there is sadness, joy.
O Divine Master,
grant that I may not so much seek
to be consoled, as to console;
to be understood, as to understand;
to be loved, as to love.
For it is in giving that we receive;
it is in pardoning that we are pardoned;
and it is in dying that
we are born to Eternal Life.
Amen

Trust in God, Not Man

While I consider the "Prayer of St. Francis" as my personal mission statement, I want to mention a scripture that I look at as foundational to my life. This scripture, reflective of Psalm 1, is Jeremiah 17:5-8; *"Thus says the Lord: Cursed is the man who trusts in man and makes flesh his arm, whose heart turns away from the Lord. He is like a shrub in the desert, and shall not see any good come. He shall dwell in the parched places of the wilderness, in an uninhabited salt land. Blessed is the man who trusts in the Lord, whose trust is the Lord. He is like a tree planted beside the water, that sends out its roots by the stream, and does not fear when heat comes, for its leaves remain green, and is not anxious in the year of drought, for it does not cease to bear fruit."*

What this scripture tells me is that when I put my trust in man and worldly things, turning my back on God, nothing good will come to me. In fact, the scripture says I will be "cursed." But it goes on to say that if I put my trust in God and depend on Him, I have absolutely nothing to fear. Regardless of the dangers I face in my life (drought), I am able to not just survive, but thrive! The world can be falling apart, but I have nothing to fear. My trust is not in the forces of this world, but in God Himself. When I live trusting in God, not man, this scripture says that I will be "blessed." In Deuteronomy, God says, *"…I have set before you life and death, blessing and curse; therefore choose life…"* (Deuteronomy 30:19) Which will you choose?

What would I do if this was Jesus?

For years now, we have seen the bracelets and the bookmarks labeled WWJD. This message is right on: "What would Jesus do?" As Christians we are asked to live like Christ. What better way for us to do that than to ask what Jesus would do in a particular situation. Once we understand what Jesus would do, we know what we are being asked to do as well.

Now I want to introduce a twist on this idea that is also extremely powerful and equally thought provoking. It is this: "What would I do if this was Jesus?" Mother Teresa of Calcutta built her entire ministry on this thought. She saw the face of Jesus in each and every person to whom she ministered. As Christians we are asked to see Jesus in each other. It is scriptural; Our Lord himself said, *"…Truly, I say to you, as you did it to one of the least of these my brethren, you did it to me."* (Matthew 25:40)

If this person is really Jesus, how will I treat him? How will I act? What will I do? What will you do?

Psalm 136: Trust In God's Love and Protection

As you read the Old Testament, you notice that whenever the nation of Israel found itself coming under attack from its many enemies, it would prepare for battle in the same way. The high priest would call all the people together and would lead them in prayer. This prayer was always the same. The priest would call upon God, and remind God and the people of all the times in Israel's history that God had delivered them from their enemies. This built up the faith of the Israelites who would enter into battle trusting that God would deliver them in the current battle just as He had delivered them in the past.

While there are many places in the Old Testament where these prayers are mentioned, Psalm 136 is one I particularly like. This psalm is a prayer of thanksgiving for God's protection of the nation of Israel. Years ago, when I first studied this psalm, I felt prompted to write my own psalm 136. I knew that I needed to do the same thing that Israel did when I faced battles in my own life. I needed to know my own personal history well enough to recall it and remember when and how God had come to my aid and saved me. This is how I build up my faith and my trust in God's love and protection. I come to see that God really does care about me personally. I see that He is intimately involved in my life! I come to know that God really does love me!

Every other line in Psalm 136 is, *"for his steadfast love endures forever."* Employing the repetition of this line made it very easy to compose my own psalm 136. I used the first verse from the original psalm to get myself going. Then I let the Holy Spirit guide me as I simply noted events that God allowed to take place in my life, starting with His choice of my parents and siblings. When I was finished, I was left with a history of my life, and interwoven through it all, *"for his steadfast love endures forever."* I cannot tell you what a powerful exercise this is! As I read my own psalm, I could feel a healing take place in my spirit. A burden I had been carrying for years was suddenly lifted from my heart. God's steadfast love had set me free!

I have recommended this exercise to many of my clients. It has produced very powerful results for anyone who takes the time to do it. I highly recommend that you do this exercise for yourself. Write your own psalm 136. Your faith will grow stronger; and you will know that you can, in fact, trust in God's love, His protection, and His provision in your life. You will come to see that His love is steadfast, and that it does, indeed, endure forever! You will come to know that God really does love you!

An Attitude of Gratitude: How To Live In Peace and Joy

"Rejoice in the Lord always; again I will say, Rejoice. Let all men know your forbearance. The Lord is at hand. Have no anxiety about anything, but in everything by prayer and supplication with thanksgiving let your requests be made known to God. And the

peace of God, which passes all understanding, will keep your hearts and minds in Christ Jesus. Finally, brethren, whatever is true, whatever is honorable, whatever is just, whatever is pure, whatever is lovely, whatever is gracious, if there is any excellence, if there is anything worthy of praise, think about these things." (Philippians 4:4-8)

This scripture passage, taken from St. Paul's letter to the Philippians, gives us a prescription for living a life of peace and joy. If we take a closer look at this scripture, we see that we are told to rejoice in God always. We are to be kind and have no fear. We are to go to God in prayer and thanksgiving and ask for what we need. If we live in this relationship of trust in God, we will have His peace and His joy in our lives. It goes on to tell us that God Himself will guard our hearts and our minds with this peace. The passage ends with what we should think about. We are to live thinking about the higher things, things of honor and beauty. We were not created to worry and fret, but to trust in God always, confident of His love for us! Remember, we were not created to get through this life under our own steam. We were created to need God in our lives. God wants us to depend on Him. He wants us to turn to Him, trusting Him completely with our lives. He wants to be God in our lives.

Scripture

The Bible is full of beautiful and powerful scriptures that inspire my life. I have chosen but a few to share with you here. I encourage you to make a list of your own favorite scriptures. While these scriptures speak to me very strongly, you will find the ones that speak to you.

Spending time every day reading and contemplating

scripture is another powerful way to grow closer to God. As Catholics, we are blessed to have daily scripture readings that go along with each day's liturgy of the Mass. Imagine, there are Catholics all around the world, in all nations and speaking all languages, that are reading and contemplating the very same scripture passages each and every day! If you are new to studying scripture, and feel a bit intimidated, this is a wonderful way to get started. Most parish bulletins publish the scripture readings for the upcoming week for those unable to attend daily Mass. These are also readily available online.

In recent years, there has been a great increase in the number of Catholic Scripture study groups that are available. Most parishes today offer some form of Bible study. If your parish does not, I am certain you will be able to find one offered in a parish nearby.

I encourage you to get into the study of scripture. I have heard the Bible described as a "love letter from God." As you draw closer in relationship to God, you will want to read His beautiful love letter. This is all part of the journey to become the person He created you to be. It is part of living *fully alive*!

Mass and Adoration

God is so abundantly generous with us. There is so much we can draw from, especially as Catholics. In addition to sacred scripture we have our sacred traditions. We have the catechism, writings of the saints, and the early church fathers. We also have the wealth of the sacraments.

As Catholics we have the privilege of daily Mass and Eucharistic Adoration. These are extremely powerful for aligning our thinking with our spirit so that we begin to live

God's will in our lives. I know in my heart that it was years of daily Mass and weekly Eucharistic Adoration that healed and shaped my life, both personally and professionally. At a time when my life was shattered, and I had no idea of how I would survive, He saved me! Slowly but surely, He guided me. Slowly but surely, I developed a deep and abiding trust in His love and mercy. What He did for me, He wants to do for you! He wants us to live leaning on Him. We were created to need Him in our lives. He wants us to trust Him completely with our lives. He wants us to become the persons He created us to be. Then we will be able to live lives that bring Him glory. We will be able to live *fully alive.*

Our Lady

As Catholics, we know that in addition to our Father in heaven, we have Mary, our mother. While we do not worship Our Lady, for she is not equal to God; we do honor her. We can also go to her to intercede with her Son on our behalf. St. Louis de Montfort says that because Mary was the means God chose to bring His Son into the world, that all graces continue to flow through her. Mary is our heavenly mother and loves us with a mother's heart.

Whenever a client has any kind of struggle with impurity, whether it is in their thoughts or actions, I point them to Our Lady. A simple "Hail Mary" prayer spoken at the time of temptation can do wonders. I have seen years of pornography addiction fall away when clients turn to Our Lady in prayer. This same healing power can bring an end to illicit relationships. As the new Eve, Our Lady crushes the head of Satan beneath her feet. At the first sound of a "Hail Mary," the devil flees!

Our Lady is also the perfect example of someone who totally trusted God with her life. At the time of the Annunciation, *"... Mary said, 'Behold, I am the handmaid of the Lord; let it be to me according to your word.'"* (Luke 1:38) With this statement to the angel, Mary gives her "fiat," her "yes," to God. From that moment on, Our Lady lives her life in total submission to God's will. Except for her son, Our Lord, Jesus, no other human being has ever brought more glory to God through her life. Our Lady certainly lived her life *fully alive*!

Prayer of Surrender to God, Our Father

Heavenly Father, I come to You today with my life in disarray. I know You created me on purpose, and have a unique purpose for my life. I know now that my life is to bring You glory. I also know that I have been living with little thought to this.
I see the confusion and chaos in my life.
So I come to You today to surrender my life to You.
I invite You into all areas of my life.

I surrender my physical being,
my health and my appearance, to You, Father.

I surrender my mind,
my thoughts and my moods, to You, Father.

I surrender my relationships,
my family and my friends, to You, Father.

I surrender my professional life, my job and my business practices, to You, Father.

It's Time to Live Your Life… Fully Alive!

I surrender my finances,
my spending and my saving, to You, Father.
I surrender my leisure time,
my fun and my entertainment, to You, Father.

Heavenly Father, You brought order and beauty out of chaos when you created the world. I ask You now, Father to do the same with my life. Please take the mess of my life and order it according to Your Holy Will for me.

Give me the courage and wisdom to live the rest of my life as a prayer of praise and thanksgiving to You.
I thank You Father, for my life,
through Jesus Christ, Our Lord.
Amen.

A Final Thought

I am so happy for you that you have begun this journey! You are entering into a wonderful process of increasing your faith and trusting in God's love for you. As you begin to trust God with your life, you will begin to live in His peace and joy. You will relax into your life, no longer fearing what others may think. You will have a greater sense of purpose with each new day. Your relationships will take on new meaning. You will sense a connection with all of God's creation. Regardless of the chaos around you, whatever your circumstances, you will be able to remain calm and still, feeling safe and secure. Your life will bring light to this dark world. Your life will bring glory to God, as you live your life *fully alive*!

Let's Stay in Touch...

I am very interested in hearing how the *Fully Alive!* program works for you. I want to hear your story! You can email me at janicecarbon@janicecarbon.com. I look forward to hearing from you.

You can also:

Subscribe to my blog, found on my website:
www.janicecarbon.com
Follow me on Twitter: @janice carbon
Like my Facebook page: Fully Alive
Follow my group board on Pinterest: Fully Alive!
(If you would like an invitation to pin on this board, simply follow the board and email me your request.)